GW00362867

Prayers for a
Quiet Heart

Kevin
Mayhew

First published in Great Britain in 1993 by
KEVIN MAYHEW LTD
Rattlesden
Bury St Edmunds
Suffolk IP30 0SZ

Lutheran Publishing House
205 Halifax Street
Adelaide
SA 5000
Australia

ISBN 0 86209 421 6

Printed in Hong Kong
by Colorcraft

CONTENTS

O LORD, my heart is not lifted up,
my eyes are not raised too high;
I do not occupy myself with things too great
and too marvellous for me.
But I have calmed and quieted my soul,
like a weaned child with its mother;
my soul is like the weaned child
that is with me.

O Israel, hope in the Lord
from this time on and for evermore.

PSALM 131

CHRIST
BE WITH ME

Christ be with me,
Christ within me,
Christ behind me,
Christ before me,
Christ beside me,
Christ to win me,
Christ to comfort
and restore me,

Christ beneath me,
Christ above me,
Christ in quiet,
Christ in danger,
Christ in hearts
of all that love me,
Christ in mouth
of friend and stranger.

I love you
with an everlasting love.

JEREMIAH 31:3

Lead me from death to life,
from falsehood to truth;
lead me from despair to hope,
from fear to trust.

Lead me from hate to love,
from war to peace;
let your peace fill our hearts,
our lives and our world.

THE GATE
OF THE YEAR

I said to the man who stood at
the gate of the year 'Give me a
light that I may tread safely
into the unknown.'
And he replied – 'Go out into the
darkness and put your hand
into the hand of God.
That shall be to you better than light
and safer than a known way!'

So I went forth and finding the
hand of God, trod gladly into
the night. And he led me
towards the hills and the
breaking of day in the lone East.

MINNIE LOUISE HASKINS

13

Where there is faith there is love,
where there is love there is peace,
and where there is peace there is God.

Lord, help me remember
that nothing is going to happen today
that you and I cannot handle together.

THE
TWENTY-THIRD PSALM

The Lord is my shepherd,
I shall not want.

He makes me lie down
in green pastures.
He leads me beside still waters;
he restores my soul.

He guides me in
paths of righteousness
for his name's sake.

Even though I walk through
the valley of the shadow of death,
I fear no evil;
for you are with me;
your rod and
your staff comfort me.

You prepare a table before me
in the presence of my enemies.
You anoint my head with oil.
My cup overflows.

Surely goodness and love
shall follow me
all the days of my life.
And I shall live
in the house of the Lord
for ever.

18

DEEP PEACE

Deep peace of the Running Wave to you.
Deep peace of the Flowing Air to you.
Deep peace of the Quiet Earth to you.
Deep peace of the Shining Stars to you.
Deep peace of the Son of Peace to you.

Martha was distracted by her many
tasks; so she came to Jesus and asked,
'Lord, do you not care that my sister has left
me to do all the work by myself? Tell her
then to help me.' But the Lord answered her,
'Martha , Martha, you are worried and
distracted by many things; there is need of
only one thing. Mary has chosen the better
part, which will not be taken away
from her.'

LUKE 10:40-42

LORD, YOUR WAY IS PERFECT

Lord, your way is perfect:
help us always to trust
in your goodness, so that,
walking with you and following you
in all simplicity,
we may possess quiet and contented minds,
and may cast all our care on you,
for you care for us.
Grant this, Lord, for your dear Son's sake,
Jesus Christ.

It is good that one should wait quietly for
the salvation of the Lord.

LAMENTATIONS 3:26

THE PEACE OF GOD

Have no anxiety about anything
but in everything,
by prayer and supplication,
with thanksgiving, let your requests
be made known to God.

And the peace of God,
which passes all understanding,
will keep your hearts and your minds
in Christ Jesus.

PHILIPPIANS 4:4-7

For thus said the Lord God,
the Holy One of Israel:
In returning and rest
you shall be saved;
in quietness and in trust
shall be your strength.

ISAIAH 30:15

Trust the past
to the mercy of God,
the present to his love,
the future to his providence.

JAMES MATTHEWS.

May your love enfold me,
may your peace surround me,
may your light touch me.

Do not look forward
to what might happen tomorrow;
the same everlasting Father
who cares for you today
will take care of you
tomorrow and every day.
Be at peace, then, and put aside
all anxious thoughts and imaginings.

FRANCIS DE SALES

Be still, and know
that I am God.

PSALM 46:10

Be at peace with one another.

MARK 9:50

THE LORD
OUR PROTECTOR

I lift up my eyes to the hills.
From whence does my help come?
My help comes from the Lord,
who made heaven and earth.

He will not let your foot be moved,
he who keeps you will not slumber.
Behold, he who keeps Israel
will neither slumber nor sleep.

The Lord is your keeper;
the Lord is your shade on your right hand.
The sun shall not smite you by day,
nor the moon by night.

The Lord will keep you from all evil;
he will keep your life.
The Lord will keep your going out and
your coming in,
from this time forth
and for evermore.

PSALM 121

PAUL'S FAREWELL

Be happy
and grow in Christ.

Do what I have said,
and live in harmony
and peace.

May the grace of our Lord
Jesus Christ
be with you all.

May God's love,
and the Holy Spirit's
friendship,
be yours.

2 CORINTHIANS 13:11-14

ACKNOWLEDGEMENTS

The publishers wishes to express their gratitude to Fine Art Photographic Library, London and th
Galleries listed below for permission to reproduce the pictures in this publication:

Front cover SPRING BLOSSOM by Otto Richter (b.1867).
Anthony Mitchell Fine Paintings, Nottingham.

Page 4 BEEHIVES IN A FLOWER GARDEN by R.T. Wilding (fl. 1895-1915).
Catto Gallery.

Page 6 INNOCENT YOUTH by Tom Mostyn (1864-1930).
Anthony Mitchell Fine Paintings, Nottingham.

Page 9 ON THE RIVER WEY, SURREY by Frederick William Hulme (1816-1884).
Galerie George.

Pages 10 &11 ROSES AND PANSIES IN A GREEK KYLIX by Johan Laurentz Jensen (1800-1856).
Verner Amell Ltd.

Page 13 POSIES by Friedrich Boser (1809-1881).
Anthony Mitchell Fine Paintings, Nottingham.

Page 15 A SUMMER GARDEN by Charles Earle (1832-1893).
Marian and John Alway, Datchet.

Page 16 & 17 THE QUAI AUX FLEURS AND THE TOUR DE L'HORLOGE
by Marie Francois Firmin-Girard (1838-1921). Galerie Berko.

Page 18 DAISIES BY THE COTTAGE DOOR by Thomas MacKay (fl. 1893-1916).
Philip Gale Gallery.

Page 21 PICKING HONEYSUCKLE by Sophie Anderson (1823-1898).

Page 22 SEPTEMBER LEAVES by Reginald Cole (1870-1940).
Nick Drummond Gallery.

Pages 24 & 25 AT MARKS GATE, ESSEX by James Matthews.
Burlington Paintings, London.

Page 26 LA LETTRE by Florent Crabeels (1829-1896).
Galerie Berko.

Page 28 INTERESTING NEWS by Marcel Hess.
Galerie Berko.

Page 30 AUTUMN by A.E. Bailey.
Bourne Gallery.